THE UL'
PCOS DIET
COOKBOOK FOR
WEIGHT LOSS AND
FERTILITY

Easy PCOS Diet to Take Control of Your Body Again: PCOS Repair Protocol to Losing Weight and Getting Pregnant

MICAELLA TERRY

Disclaimer

The meal plan and information presented in this content are the result of extensive research and are intended for general informational purposes only. They do not constitute professional medical advice, diagnosis, or treatment. It is highly recommended that you consult with a healthcare professional or registered dietitian before embarking on any new diet, exercise program, or making changes to your existing healthcare regimen, especially if you have specific medical conditions or concerns, including PCOS. Individual results and experiences may vary.

Always prioritize your health and well-being by seeking the guidance of qualified professionals.

CONTENTS

Introduction

Welcome to the Ultimate PCOS Diet Cookbook for Weight Loss and Fertility! For over 20 years, I have been passionate about helping women with Polycystic Ovary Syndrome (PCOS) find relief and reclaim their health. This cookbook is the culmination of my experience, research, and culinary creativity, designed to help you manage PCOS symptoms, lose weight, and improve fertility.

PCOS is a complex hormonal disorder that affects millions of women worldwide. It often causes weight gain, infertility, and a variety of other health issues. A well-balanced, nutrient-dense diet tailored to your unique needs is a crucial part of managing PCOS and restoring your body's natural balance.

Throughout this cookbook, I will guide you on a journey of discovery, as you learn about the foods that will help alleviate your PCOS symptoms and those that you should avoid. You will find a collection of delicious, easy-to-follow recipes for breakfast, lunch, and dinner, as well as snacks and beverages, all designed to support weight loss and improve fertility.

Each recipe includes short, easy-to-understand instructions, as well as tips for customizing the dish to suit your tastes and preferences. I have ensured that this cookbook is valuable, rich in content, and concise, allowing you to quickly find the information and recipes you need.

Get ready to embark on a life-changing journey toward optimal health and fertility with the *Ultimate PCOS Diet Cookbook*! Let's dive into the delicious world of PCOS-friendly meals and explore how simple dietary changes can make a significant difference in your life.

Understanding PCOS and Its Impact on Fertility

Polycystic Ovary Syndrome (PCOS) is a common hormonal disorder that affects 1 in 10 women of reproductive age. It is characterized by insulin resistance, elevated androgen levels (male hormones), and irregular menstrual cycles. These hormonal imbalances can lead to a variety of symptoms, including weight gain, acne, excessive hair growth, and fertility issues.

Women with PCOS often struggle with ovulation problems, making it

challenging to conceive. However, by
managing PCOS through diet and

lifestyle changes, many women can improve their fertility and increase their chances of becoming pregnant.

The Role of Diet in Managing PCOS

Diet plays a crucial role in managing PCOS symptoms and improving fertility. A well-balanced, nutrient-dense diet can help regulate insulin levels, reduce inflammation, and support hormonal balance. This, in turn, can promote weight loss, improve menstrual regularity, and boost fertility.

When it comes to a PCOS-friendly diet, the focus should be on whole, unprocessed foods. These include lean proteins, healthy fats, high-fiber carbohydrates, and plenty of fruits and vegetables. Avoiding refined sugars, processed foods, and excessive caffeine is also essential for optimal results.

Top 10 Foods to Include in Your PCOS Diet

i. Leafy greens
ii. Fatty fish (e.g., salmon, mackerel)
iii. Nuts and seeds
iv. Whole grains (e.g., quinoa, brown rice)
v. Berries
vi. Legumes (e.g., lentils, chickpeas)
vii. Avocado
viii. Extra virgin olive oil
ix. Lean protein (e.g., chicken, turkey)
x. Greek yogurt

Top 10 Foods to Avoid with PCOS

i. Refined sugars and high-fructose corn syrup

ii. Processed foods

iii. Saturated and trans fats

iv. Caffeine in excess

v. Alcohol

vi. Refined carbohydrates (e.g., white bread, pasta)

vii. High-GI fruits (e.g., pineapple, watermelon)

viii. Artificial sweeteners

ix. Soy products (in excess)

x. Red and processed meats

Meal Planning for PCOS Weight Loss and Fertility

Creating a meal plan tailored to your unique needs and preferences is essential for managing PCOS symptoms, losing weight, and improving fertility. This cookbook provides you with a variety of delicious, PCOS-friendly recipes to choose from, making it easy to create a meal plan that suits your lifestyle and goals.

When planning your meals, consider the following tips:

1. **Focus on balance:** Aim for a mix of lean proteins, healthy fats, and high-fiber carbohydrates in each meal.

2. **Practice portion control:** Avoid overeating by using smaller plates and serving sizes.

3. **Prioritize nutrient-dense foods:** Choose whole, unprocessed foods that are rich in vitamins, minerals, and antioxidants.

4. **Stay hydrated:** Drink plenty of water throughout the day to support digestion and overall health.

5. **Plan ahead:** Prepare meals and snacks in advance to avoid making unhealthy choices when you're short on time.

With these tips in mind, you can create a meal plan that supports your PCOS management goals and helps you achieve a healthy, balanced lifestyle.

Breakfast Recipes

Green Smoothie Bowl:

Blend 1 cup of spinach, 1/2 cup of frozen mixed berries, 1/2 banana, 1/2 cup almond milk, and 1 scoop of protein powder. Pour into a bowl and top with sliced fruits, nuts, and chia seeds.

Almond Butter and Chia Seed Overnight Oats:

Combine 1/2 cup rolled oats, 1 tbsp chia seeds, 1 tbsp almond butter, 1 cup almond milk, and 1/2 tsp vanilla extract in a jar. Refrigerate overnight. Top with sliced almonds and fresh berries before serving.

Veggie-Packed Frittata:

Sauté chopped onion, bell peppers, and spinach in a non-stick skillet. Whisk 8 eggs with salt and pepper, pour over the vegetables, and cook until set. Top with crumbled feta cheese and finish under the broiler.

Spinach and Mushroom Egg Muffins:

Sauté chopped mushrooms and spinach in a non-stick skillet. Whisk 8 eggs with salt and pepper. Divide the vegetables into a greased muffin tin, pour the egg mixture over the top, and bake at 350°F for 20-25 minutes.

Quinoa Breakfast Porridge with Berries:
Cook 1/2 cup quinoa in 1 cup almond milk with a pinch of salt. Simmer until tender. Stir in 1/2 tsp vanilla extract and 1 tbsp maple syrup. Top with fresh berries and a dollop of Greek yogurt.

Greek Yogurt Parfait with Nuts and Seeds:
Layer 1 cup Greek yogurt, 1/4 cup granola, a handful of mixed nuts, and fresh berries in a glass. Drizzle with honey or maple syrup.

Avocado Toast with Smoked Salmon:

Mash 1/2 avocado with salt and pepper. Spread on a slice of whole-grain toast. Top with smoked salmon, thinly sliced red onion, and a sprinkle of capers.

Protein-Packed Pancakes:
Blend 1 cup oats, 1 banana, 2 eggs, 1/2 cup Greek yogurt, and 1 tsp baking

powder. Cook spoonfuls of batter on a non-stick griddle over medium heat. Flip when bubbles appear. Serve with fresh fruit and a drizzle of maple syrup.

Cottage Cheese and Fruit Bowl:
In a bowl, combine 1 cup cottage cheese, 1/2 cup sliced strawberries, and 1/4 cup blueberries. Top with a drizzle of honey and a sprinkle of chopped nuts.

Shakshuka with Whole Grain Toast:
Sauté chopped onion, bell pepper, and garlic in a skillet. Stir in 1 can of diced tomatoes, 1 tsp paprika, 1/2 tsp cumin, and salt to taste. Simmer until thickened. Make 4 wells in the sauce and crack an egg into each. Cook until the egg whites are set. Serve with whole-grain toast.

Lunch Recipes

Grilled Chicken Salad with Avocado Dressing:

Grill a seasoned chicken breast until cooked through. Slice and serve on a bed of mixed greens, cherry tomatoes, and cucumber. Blend 1 avocado, juice of 1 lime, 1/4 cup Greek yogurt, and salt to taste for the dressing. Drizzle over salad.

Lentil and Vegetable Soup:
Sauté chopped onion, carrots, and celery in a pot. Stir in 1 cup lentils, 6 cups vegetable broth, and 1 can diced tomatoes. Season with salt, pepper, and thyme. Simmer until lentils are tender. Stir in chopped kale and cook until wilted.

Chickpea and Quinoa Buddha Bowl:
Combine cooked quinoa, roasted chickpeas, sliced avocado, chopped kale, cherry tomatoes, and cucumber in a bowl. Drizzle with a lemon-tahini dressing.

Zucchini Noodles with Pesto and Cherry Tomatoes:

Spiralize 2 zucchinis into noodles. Sauté cherry tomatoes in a skillet until softened. Toss with zucchini noodles and 1/4 cup pesto. Serve warm or chilled.

Turkey and Hummus Lettuce Wraps:

Spread hummus on large lettuce leaves. Layer with sliced turkey, tomato, and cucumber. Roll up and enjoy.

Mediterranean Stuffed Bell Peppers:

Stuff halved bell peppers with a mixture of cooked quinoa, chopped spinach, crumbled feta, and chopped olives. Bake at 375°F for 25-30 minutes, or until peppers are tender.

Cauliflower Fried Rice with Shrimp:

Sauté shrimp, garlic, and ginger in a skillet until shrimp are cooked. Set aside. Pulse cauliflower florets in a food processor until rice-like. Sauté with diced carrots, peas, and onion in the skillet. Stir in cooked shrimp, soy sauce, and scrambled eggs.

Roasted Vegetable and Feta Salad:

Toss chopped bell peppers, zucchini, red onion, and cherry tomatoes in olive oil, salt, and pepper. Roast at 425°F for 20-25 minutes. Serve over mixed greens with crumbled feta and a balsamic vinaigrette.

Spicy Black Bean and Sweet Potato Tacos:

Sauté cubed sweet potatoes with a pinch of cumin and chili powder. Stir in black beans and cook until heated through. Serve in corn tortillas with avocado, salsa, and cilantro.

Tuna-Stuffed Avocado Boats:

Mix 1 can of tuna with 1/4 cup diced red onion, 1/4 cup diced celery, 2 tbsp Greek yogurt, and salt to taste. Spoon mixture into halved avocados and garnish with chopped chives.

Dinner Recipes

Baked Lemon Herb Salmon with Asparagus:

Season salmon fillet with lemon juice, olive oil, minced garlic, salt, and pepper. Place on a baking sheet with trimmed asparagus. Bake at 400°F for 12-15 minutes, or until salmon is cooked through and asparagus is tender.

Stuffed Eggplant with Ground Turkey and Quinoa:
Scoop out the flesh of halved eggplants, leaving a 1/4-inch shell. Brown ground turkey in a skillet and mix with cooked quinoa, diced tomatoes, and chopped eggplant flesh. Fill eggplant shells with the mixture and bake at 375°F for 25-30 minutes.

Chicken and Vegetable Stir-Fry:
Sauté diced chicken breast in a skillet until cooked through. Add chopped bell peppers, broccoli, and snap peas. Stir in a sauce made from soy sauce, honey, and cornstarch. Serve over cooked brown rice.

Spaghetti Squash Bolognese:

Roast halved spaghetti squash at 400°F for 40-45 minutes. Sauté ground beef, onion, and garlic in a skillet. Stir in canned crushed tomatoes, basil, and oregano. Simmer for 20 minutes. Shred cooked spaghetti squash with a fork and top with Bolognese sauce.

Slow Cooker Moroccan Lentil Stew:
Combine 1 cup lentils, 1 can diced tomatoes, 1 chopped onion, 2 diced carrots, 3 cups vegetable broth, and spices (cumin, coriander, cinnamon, and paprika) in a slow cooker. Cook on low for 6-8 hours or high for 4-6 hours. Stir in chopped kale before serving.

Baked Chicken Parmesan with Zucchini Noodles:
Dip chicken breasts in beaten egg, then in a mixture of breadcrumbs and grated Parmesan. Bake at 400°F for 20-25 minutes, or until cooked through. Serve over sautéed zucchini noodles with marinara sauce.

One-Pan Pesto Chicken and Vegetables:

Place seasoned chicken breasts, halved cherry tomatoes, and green beans on a baking sheet. Drizzle with olive oil and pesto. Bake at 400°F for 20-25 minutes, or until chicken is cooked through and vegetables are tender.

Cauliflower Crust Pizza with Veggie Toppings:

Combine riced cauliflower, 1 egg, and 1/4 cup shredded mozzarella. Press into a pizza crust on a lined baking sheet. Bake at 425°F for 20 minutes. Add marinara sauce, cheese, and sliced vegetables. Bake for another 10-15 minutes.

Thai Coconut Curry with Tofu and Vegetables:

Sauté cubed tofu, chopped bell peppers, and sliced zucchini in a skillet. Stir in a mixture of coconut milk, red curry paste, soy sauce, and lime juice. Simmer until vegetables are tender. Serve over cooked brown rice.

Turkey and Vegetable Stuffed Peppers:
Stuff halved bell peppers with a mixture of cooked ground turkey, chopped zucchini, diced tomatoes, and cooked brown rice. Season with salt, pepper, and oregano. Bake at 350°F for 30-35 minutes, or until peppers are tender.

Snack and Dessert Recipes

i.   Apple Slices with Almond Butter

ii.   Greek Yogurt and Fruit Popsicles

iii.   Roasted Chickpeas with Spices

iv.   Dark Chocolate and Nut Energy Bites

v.   Carrot Sticks with Homemade Hummus

vi.   Chia Seed Pudding with Fresh Berries

vii.   Baked Kale Chips

viii.   Cucumber and Cottage Cheese Bites

ix.   Homemade Trail Mix

x.   Coconut Macaroons with Dark Chocolate Drizzle

Beverages for PCOS

i. Infused Water (e.g., cucumber, lemon, or berries)

ii. Herbal Teas (e.g., green tea, peppermint, chamomile)

iii. Freshly Squeezed Vegetable and Fruit Juices

iv. Protein Smoothies (e.g., spinach, almond milk, and protein powder)

v. Golden Milk (turmeric-based warm beverage)

Lifestyle Tips for PCOS Management

In addition to a well-balanced diet, adopting healthy lifestyle habits can further support your PCOS management goals. Consider incorporating the following tips:

i. **Regular exercise:** Aim for at least 30 minutes of moderate-intensity exercise most days of the week.

ii. **Stress management:** Practice relaxation techniques such as deep breathing, meditation, or yoga.

iii. **Sleep hygiene:** Prioritize 7-9 hours of quality sleep each night and maintain a consistent sleep schedule.

iv. **Support network:** Connect with others who have PCOS through support groups, online forums, or local meet-ups.

v. **Work with healthcare professionals:** Collaborate with your healthcare team to develop a personalized plan to manage your PCOS symptoms and improve fertility.

Conclusion

With the ultimate PCOS cookbook for weight loss and fertility in hand, you now have the tools, knowledge, and recipes to make meaningful changes in your diet and lifestyle. By following these guidelines and incorporating the delicious PCOS-friendly recipes, you can take charge of your health, manage your symptoms, and improve your fertility.

2-Weeks Meal Plan

Week 1:
Day 1:

Breakfast: Green Smoothie Bowl

Lunch: Grilled Chicken Salad with Avocado Dressing

Dinner: Baked Lemon Herb Salmon with Asparagus

Snack: Apple Slices with Almond Butter

Day 2:

Breakfast: Almond Butter and Chia Seed Overnight Oats

Lunch: Lentil and Vegetable Soup

Dinner: Stuffed Eggplant with Ground Turkey and Quinoa

Snack: Greek Yogurt and Fruit Popsicles

Day 3:

Breakfast: Veggie-Packed Frittata

Lunch: Chickpea and Quinoa Buddha Bowl

Dinner: Chicken and Vegetable Stir-Fry

Snack: Roasted Chickpeas with Spices

Day 4:

Breakfast: Spinach and Mushroom Egg Muffins

Lunch: Zucchini Noodles with Pesto and Cherry Tomatoes

Dinner: Spaghetti Squash Bolognese

Snack: Dark Chocolate and Nut Energy Bites

Day 5:

Breakfast: Quinoa Breakfast Porridge with Berries

Lunch: Turkey and Hummus Lettuce Wraps

Dinner: Slow Cooker Moroccan Lentil Stew

Snack: Carrot Sticks with Homemade Hummus

Day 6:

Breakfast: Greek Yogurt Parfait with Nuts and Seeds

Lunch: Mediterranean Stuffed Bell Peppers

Dinner: Baked Chicken Parmesan with Zucchini Noodles

Snack: Chia Seed Pudding with Fresh Berries

Day 7:

Breakfast: Avocado Toast with Smoked Salmon

Lunch: Cauliflower Fried Rice with Shrimp

Dinner: One-Pan Pesto Chicken and Vegetables

Snack: Baked Kale Chips

Week 2:
Day 1:

Breakfast: Protein-Packed Pancakes

Lunch: Roasted Vegetable and Feta Salad

Dinner: Cauliflower Crust Pizza with Veggie Toppings

Snack: Cucumber and Cottage Cheese Bites

Day 2:

Breakfast: Cottage Cheese and Fruit Bowl

Lunch: Spicy Black Bean and Sweet Potato Tacos

Dinner: Thai Coconut Curry with Tofu and Vegetables

Snack: Homemade Trail Mix

Day 3:

Breakfast: Shakshuka with Whole Grain Toast

Lunch: Tuna-Stuffed Avocado Boats

Dinner: Turkey and Vegetable Stuffed Peppers

Snack: Coconut Macaroons with Dark Chocolate Drizzle

Day 4:

Breakfast: Green Smoothie Bowl

Lunch: Grilled Chicken Salad with Avocado Dressing

Dinner: Baked Lemon Herb Salmon with Asparagus

Snack: Apple Slices with Almond Butter

Day 5:

Breakfast: Almond Butter and Chia Seed Overnight Oats

Lunch: Lentil and Vegetable Soup

Dinner: Stuffed Eggplant with Ground Turkey and Quinoa

Snack: Greek Yogurt and Fruit Popsicles

Day 6:

Breakfast: Veggie-Packed Frittata

Lunch: Chickpea and Quinoa Buddha Bowl

Dinner: Chicken and Vegetable Stir-Fry

Snack: Roasted Chickpeas with Spices

Day 7:

Breakfast: Spinach and Mushroom Egg Muffins

Lunch: Zucchini Noodles with Pesto and Cherry Tomatoes

Dinner: Spaghetti Squash Bolognese

Snack: Dark Chocolate and Nut Energy Bites

Shopping List

Fruits: bananas, mixed berries, apples, strawberries, blueberries, lemons, limes, avocados, tomatoes, cherries

Vegetables: spinach, kale, asparagus, bell peppers, zucchini, eggplant, onions, garlic, carrots, celery, peas, green beans, cauliflower

Grains: oats, quinoa, whole-grain bread, spaghetti squash, brown rice, corn tortillas

Proteins: chicken breasts, ground turkey, salmon, shrimp, tofu, eggs, Greek yogurt, cottage cheese, tuna, turkey slices, almonds, hummus

Dairy: feta cheese, mozzarella cheese, almond milk, Parmesan cheese

Pantry: chia seeds, canned chickpeas, lentils, canned tomatoes, tomato sauce, pesto, red curry paste, coconut milk, soy sauce, honey, maple syrup, dark chocolate, breadcrumbs, almond butter, tahini, nuts, seeds

Spices and herbs: salt, pepper, thyme, basil, oreg ry, oregano, cumin, coriander, cinnamon, paprika, curry paste, ginger, capers, vanilla extract, red pepper flakes

Oils and vinegars: olive oil, balsamic vinegar, coconut oil

Miscellaneous: protein powder, baking powder, cornstarch

This 2-week meal plan and shopping list will provide a variety of delicious and nutritious meals for breakfast, lunch, dinner, and snacks. The recipes are designed with PCOS in mind, focusing on whole foods, lean proteins, and low-glycemic carbohydrates to help balance hormones, manage weight, and improve fertility. Enjoy these meals as part of a healthy lifestyle to better manage your PCOS symptoms.

Printed in Great Britain
by Amazon